WHAT SHOULD I DO? WHAT SHOULD I DO? WHAT SHOULD I DO? WHAT SHOULD I DO? WHAT SHOULD I DO? WHAT SHOULD I DO?

WHAT SHOULD I DO?
IF I SEE A STRAY ANIMAL

BY WIL MARA

Published in the United States of America by Cherry Lake Publishing
Ann Arbor, Michigan
www.cherrylakepublishing.com

Content Adviser: Karen Sheehan, MD, MPH, Children's Memorial Hospital, Chicago, Illinois

Photo Credits: Cover and page 1, ©Lane V. Erickson/Shutterstock, Inc.; page 5, ©Tina Rencelj/Shutterstock, Inc.; page 7, ©saiko3p/Shutterstock, Inc.; page 9, ©Art_man/Shutterstock, Inc.; page 11, ©Viktor Gladkov/Shutterstock, Inc.; page 13, ©Goodluz/Shutterstock, Inc.; page 15, ©Studio 1One/Shutterstock, Inc.; page 17, ©Pam Mamsch; page 19, ©Scott Rothstein/Shutterstock, Inc.; page 21, ©Seiji/Shutterstock, Inc.

LIBRARY OF CONGRESS CATALOGING-IN-PUBLICATION DATA
Mara, Wil.
  What should I do? I see a stray animal/by Wil Mara.
    p. cm.—(Community connections)
  Includes bibliographical references and index.
  ISBN-13: 978-1-61080-050-1 (lib. bdg.)
  ISBN-10: 1-61080-050-8 (lib. bdg.)
  1. Feral animals—Juvenile literature. 2. Feral dogs—Juvenile literature.
  3. Feral cats—Juvenile literature. 4. Safety education—Juvenile literature.
  5. Public safety—Juvenile literature. I.Title. II. Series.
  SF140.F47M37 2011
  613.6—dc22   2010053753

Cherry Lake Publishing would like to acknowledge the work of The Partnership for 21st Century Skills. Please visit *www.21stcenturyskills.org* for more information.

Printed in the United States of America
Corporate Graphics Inc.
July 2011
CLFA09

IF I SEE A STRAY ANIMAL

CONTENTS

WHAT SHOULD I DO?

NOT ALWAYS YOUR FRIEND

Pets can make you very happy. It is a lot of fun to play with a dog or a cat. But not all animals are your friends.

Stray animals can be very dangerous. Do you know what to do if you see one outside?

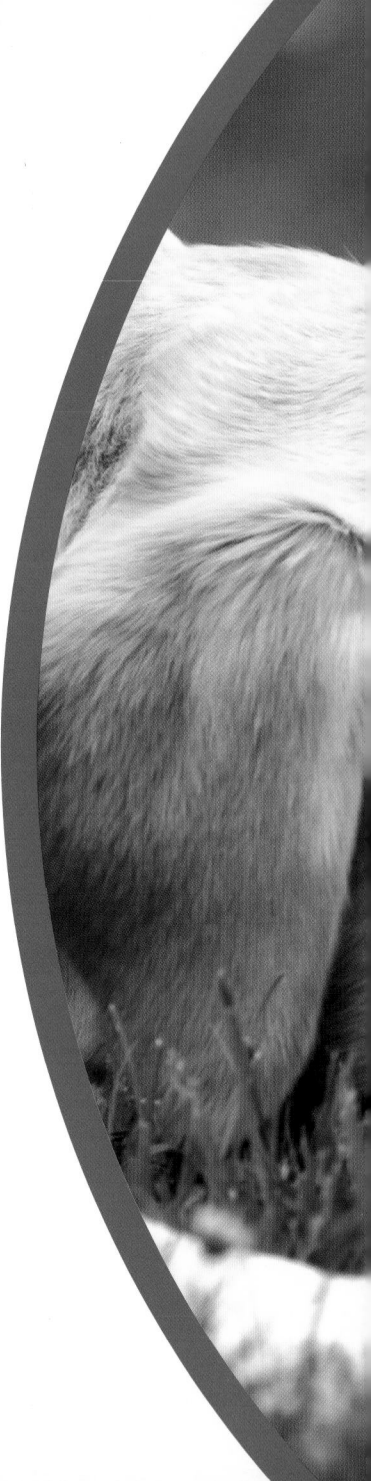

4

Do you know the pets in your neighborhood?

ASK QUESTIONS!

Get to know your neighbors' pets. Find out their names. Learn if they are friendly or not. You should always know which animals are your neighbors' pets and which ones are strays.

5

HELPING THEM COULD HURT YOU

You might want to go near a stray animal if you see one. Maybe you think it is lost. You might want to bring it back home. Or maybe it looks hungry and you want to feed it. These are all bad ideas.

Feeding stray animals can be dangerous.

7

Stray animals can be very mean. Even those that look friendly could scratch or bite you.

Sometimes stray animals are sick. Some have a **disease** called **rabies**. You can catch rabies, too, if an animal scratches or bites you. It will make you very sick.

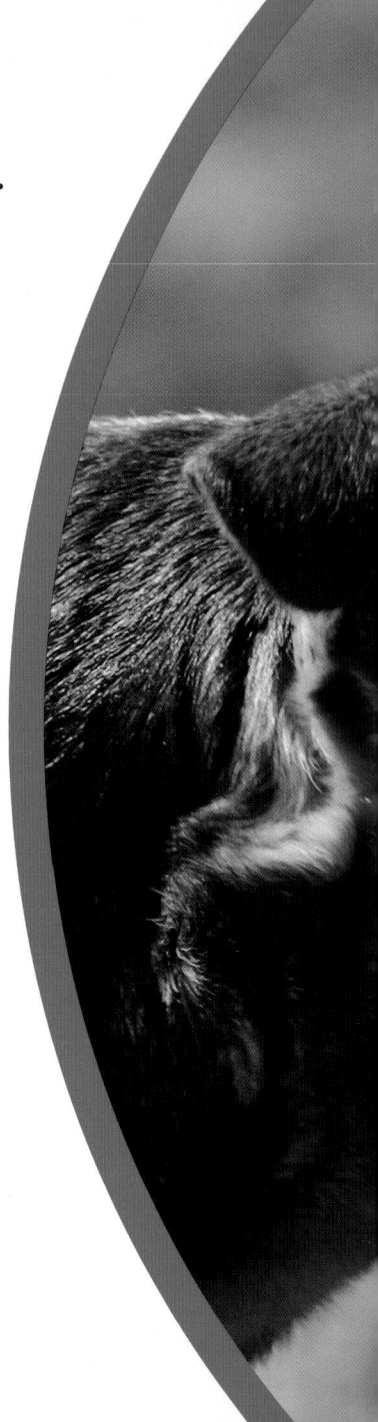

8

Stray animals can bite or scratch you.

LOOK!

There are some clues that will help you figure out if an animal is sick. It will walk slowly. It may hiss or growl. Sometimes it will have foam coming out of its mouth. Call for help if you see an animal like this—and don't go near it!

9

WHAT YOU SHOULD DO

There are some rules you should always follow when you see a stray animal. The most important rule is to never go near the animal. Do not try to feed it or pet it. Stay as far away from it as you can.

10

The best thing to do if you see a stray animal is to stay far away from it.

Slowly walk away from the animal. Walk backward so you can keep an eye on the animal while you are walking away. Make sure it does not come after you.

Try to get inside your house or a friend's house. Then call an adult for help. You can also call **9-1-1** or **animal control**.

If you don't know how to call 9-1-1, have an adult show you what to do.

CREATE!

Make a list of emergency phone numbers. One of them should be for your local animal control office. Another should be for a neighbor who can help you if your parents are out. What other numbers might be good to write down?

13

You might think you should run away from a stray animal if it comes close by you. Do not do this. Be very still instead. The animal might come up and smell you. But then it will probably go away.

Do not make any loud noises, either. Noise or fast movement could scare the animal. A scared animal might bite you.

Running away from a stray animal is not a good idea. It might chase you.

15

Curl up into a tight ball if a stray animal knocks you down. Cover your head with your arms. Pull your knees up to your chest. Do not move once you are curled up. The stray animal should leave you alone after a while.

Stay still, cover your head, and make yourself as small as possible if a stray animal knocks you down.

IF YOU ARE BITTEN OR SCRATCHED

Change your clothes and take a bath or shower as soon as possible if a stray animal touches you. Do not eat anything or put your hands in your mouth until you are clean. Stray animals often have **germs** that can make you sick.

If a stray animal touches you, take a shower or bath to wash away germs.

Find an adult right away
if you are scratched or bitten.
You need to have your cuts cleaned.
Then the adult should call a
doctor. You might also have to go
to the **hospital**.

Many animals are fun to be
around. Follow the rules so you
don't have to be afraid of them!

You will stay safe if you keep away from stray
animals, even the ones that look cute.

Why do you think stray animals might try to hurt people? Could they be scared? Maybe they are confused. They might think you are trying to hurt them. What else might cause a stray animal to attack?

21

GLOSSARY

animal control (AN-uh-muhl kuhn-TROL) a group of people who deal with dangerous animals

disease (di-ZEEZ) sickness

germs (JURMZ) tiny living things that can make you sick

hospital (HAHS-pi-tull) a place where very sick people receive medical attention

9-1-1 (NINE WUHN WUHN) a special phone number you can call to get help during emergencies

rabies (RAY-beez) a deadly disease carried by animals and that can be passed to people

stray (STRAY) without a home

FIND OUT MORE

BOOKS

Klosterman, Lorrie. *Rabies*. Tarrytown, NY: Marshall Cavendish Benchmark, 2008.

Payne, Renee. *Be a Dog's Best Friend: A Safety Guide for Kids*. Brooklyn, NY: Doggie Couch Books, 2009.

WEB SITES

Growing Up with Pets—Safety Tips for Kids from the AKC
www.growingupwithpets.com/just_for_kids/en/safety_tips.shtml
Learn how to stay safe around dogs.

KidsHealth—How to Stay Safe Around Animals
kidshealth.org/kid/watch/house/animals.html
Check out some tips for staying safe around strays, wild animals, and pets.

INDEX

ABOUT THE AUTHOR

Wil Mara is the award-winning author of more than 120 books, many of which are educational titles for children. More information about his work can be found at *www.wilmara.com.*

24